STRONG *IN* TRIALS AND TRIBULATIONS

Doc Murphy

Doc Murphy Movements

Plano, Texas

Copyright © 2020-2025 by Doc Murphy.

3rd Edition

All rights reserved. No part of this book may be reproduced or transmitted in any form or by any means, electronic or mechanical, including photocopying, recording, or by any information storage and retrieval system, without permission in writing from the copyright owner.

Unless otherwise indicated, all Scripture quotations are taken from the King James Version of the Bible.

Some scripture quotations are the author's paraphrase.

This book was printed in the United States of America.

Doc Murphy Movements

2220 Coit Rd. Ste 480-123

Plano, Tx. 75075

Published by Everywhere Publishing

ISBN: 9798674674337

For Booking and to order additional copies of this book, contact:

Doc Murphy Movements | The Everywhere Network

pastordocmurphy@gmail.com

www.docmurphy.net

CONTENTS

Introduction: 8

1. The reason we go through hardship...............15
2. Maximum Joy!..27
3. Let Patience Work......................................36
4. The Job Syndrome.....................................40
5. The Trial of Your Faith..............................53

ABOUT THE AUTHOR...............59

PRODUCTS............................60

Appendix............................63

BEFORE WE GET STARTED…

Before we get started, let me be clear—this book isn't about God's judgment against wicked people or those who disobey Him and refuse to repent. This book is about **how to be strong in the trials that the devil sends.**

God has allowed evil (calamity) to come upon the wicked. There is a difference between the wicked and those who truly follow God and His righteous ways. You don't see the righteous being judged by God with calamity—you see them being attacked by the *devil*. But God gives His people power to overcome the attacks of the devil. *This* is what this book is about.

Many have confused God's judgment on evil people and His people who refuse to obey Him with the devil's attacks against God's people who live holy before Him. Before we go deeper into this book, I'd like to explain a verse in the Bible that has confused many:

Isaiah 45:7 (KJV)
"I form the light, and create darkness: I make peace, and create evil: I the LORD do all these things."

The Hebrew Breakdown
Let's examine the Hebrew words used in this verse—particularly the one that raises eyebrows: "evil."

- **"Form"** = *yatsar (יָצַר)*: to shape, fashion, mold like a potter.
- **"Create"** = *bara (בָּרָא)*: to bring into existence (used in Genesis 1).
- **"Light"** = *or (אוֹר)*: illumination, brightness.
- **"Darkness"** = *choshek (חֹשֶׁךְ)*: obscurity, gloom, the absence of light.
- **"Peace"** = *shalom (שָׁלוֹם)*: wholeness, completeness, prosperity, harmony.
- **"Evil"** = *ra (רַע)*: This word can mean moral evil, but also **calamity, disaster**, distress, or trouble—**depending on the context.**

Clarifying "I create evil"
The KJV uses the word "evil," but many modern translations interpret it as:

- "I bring calamity" (NKJV, NASB)
- "I create disaster" (NIV, ESV)

Why the difference? Because in the Hebrew context, *ra* in this verse **doesn't mean moral sin or wickedness, but rather disaster or judgment**. It's not saying God is the author of sin—it's declaring that He is sovereign over both blessing and judgment, peace and calamity.

Rick Renner, known for his word studies and deep dives into Greek and Hebrew, emphasizes that God is *not* the source of moral evil. However, He does allow or even **commission judgment** as part of His sovereign justice. He explains:

- God sometimes uses disruption or calamity to wake up nations or individuals.
- God doesn't commit sin or tempt people to do evil (James 1:13), but He may orchestrate events that include hardship to fulfill judge wickedness.
- The word "evil" here is best understood as catastrophe or calamity—not moral perversion.

This verse speaks to the *absolute righteousness* of God.

It's a comfort to the righteous and a warning to the rebellious. God is not passive. He uses *all* things—even calamity against the wicked.

- **Amos 3:6** – "Shall there be evil in a city, and the Lord hath not done it?" (*again, "evil" means calamity*)

Isaiah 45:7 is *not* a contradiction of God's goodness—it's a revelation of His power and justice. He doesn't commit sin, but He reigns over His judgment and consequences. In a chaotic world, this verse brings comfort. The righteous are protected and the wicked get judged.

INTRODUCTION

You can be strong *in* trials and tribulations. I didn't say be strong **BECAUSE of** trials. No, be strong *in* them. You should be strong **before** the trials come so you can overcome them. The strength that the **grace of God gives** will not only allow you to be strong in the trial but also help you to overcome it.

2 Timothy 2:1 <u>New Living Translation</u> Timothy, my dear son, be strong through the grace that God gives you in Christ Jesus.

2 Timothy 2:1 <u>English Standard Version</u> You then, my child, be strengthened by the grace that is in Christ Jesus,

Notice the strength doesn't come from trials; it comes from Christ. It comes from His grace.

The reason I'm hammering that point is that many believe that the trials come to make them strong. The reason for this line of thinking is because they believe God sent the trial, testing, or tribulation. This is inaccurate. The trials, testing, or tribulation were sent by the Devil to weaken the believer. Problems come to make you weak. God has many ways to make you strong, and they don't involve using trials and tribulations. *God doesn't need Satan's evil to help build you up.* God doesn't use what the Devil uses to grow you spiritually. The thought of that is ridiculous!

Note: We will discuss the "testing" of the Lord in a later Chapter

Look at what Jesus says about tribulation:

John 16:33 I have told you these things so that in Me you may have peace. In the world, you will have tribulation. But take courage; I have overcome the world!"

Ok, let's break down what Jesus said:

- **Tribulation** is the SAME word for trials, sorrow, trouble, testing, and suffering.

- **Take Courage** is the same as saying, "Take Heart," "Don't worry," "Be of Good Cheer," or "Be cheerful."

- **I have Overcome** means to prevail or conquer.

- ***World*** means *"ordered system."* It's the system of how the sinful world operates. Part of this order is tribulation.

Jesus says, *"in the world (the ordered system), you will have trials, testing, sufferings, trouble, tribulation, sorrow. But take courage, take heart, don't worry about it, be full of cheer, get glad, because I have overcome the world."*

We are in Christ, and therefore we have the same victory He has. Our faith gives us the victory over the world; in which trials, tribulations, troubles, suffering, and sorrow come.

1 John 5:4 for everyone born of God overcomes the world. <u>This is the victory that has overcome the world, even our faith.</u>

Jesus didn't send the tribulations or trials (evil testings). Those things come from the world *(and Satan is the God of this world-ordered system. 2 Cor 4:4),* and we are overcomers of the world as Jesus is. Also, notice Jesus didn't say the tribulation was coming to make them strong. No, He knows what difficulties do to people, or He would not have said,

"Take courage." He was saying the tribulation is a BAD thing, and this is something you must overcome by overcoming the whole ordered system (world).

If we can get people to stop operating as the world does (by helping them to renew their minds), then they can overcome it. You must Love NOT the world (the system). The system only brings heartache, pain, suffering, trials, testing, tribulations, persecution, lies, sin, poverty, and all other kinds of evil. We are not to live according to the world's standards. When you see people accepting trials and tribulations as the will of God, they are simply *"Worldly."* Their minds haven't been renewed. They still love the world's operation.

You can't overcome what you tolerate, celebrate, participate in, and anticipate.

Many Christians anticipate the world's system to happen to them *as the will of God*, and they participate in the activities of the ordered system. This is why many live defeated and never experience the power of God.

1 John 2: [15] **Love not the world, neither the things that are in the world.** *If any man loves the world, the* *love of the Father is not in him. ⁶¹ For all that is in the world, the lust of the flesh, and the lust of the eyes, and the pride of life, is not of the Father but is of the world. ⁷¹ And the world passeth away, and the lust thereof: but he that doeth the will of God abideth for ever.*

Romans 12:2 and **be not conformed (fashioned) to this world***: but be ye* **transformed by the renewing of your mind,** *that ye may prove what that good is, and acceptable, and perfect, will of God.*

We are commanded as believers not to love the world or pattern our lives after its way of doing things. The ordered system is corrupt and dangerous for the Believer. We should not befriend it. We love the people of the world, and yes, we can be friends with the people. But **we do not participate** in what they do or the "ordered system."

2 Peter 1:4 Through these he has given us his very great and precious promises, so that through them you may participate in the divine nature, **having escaped the corruption in the world caused by evil desires.**

James 4:4 You adulterous people, don't you know that friendship with the world means enmity against God? Therefore, **anyone who chooses to be a friend of the world becomes an enemy of God.**

So we can see that tribulation comes from the world. Jesus overcame or conquered the ordered system, which means that <u>He overcame hardship (testing, trials, suffering, sorrow, trouble).</u> He proves that over and over again throughout His years on the earth. As we follow His example and stop blaming God for the tribulation, we too will conquer, dominate, and master the ordered system.

BE STRONG!

You get strength from the Lord, the Word, grace, joy, and the Spirit (not storms or trials). You are STRONG in your spirit and mind. You are tough! Don't fall for this mental issue business; where they celebrate people for being defeated and weak. We are commanded to be strong. God said to ***"BE STRONG".*** You have strength in you. Stop talking "weakness" and start talking "strength". **You have a strong mind! It's OK to be OK!**

Joshua 1:7 ***<u>Be strong</u>*** and very courageous.

Ephesians 6:10 A final word: ***<u>Be strong in the Lord</u>***

and in his mighty power.

2 Tim 2:1 You then, my son, **_be strong in the grace_** that is in Christ Jesus.

Ephesians 3:16 That he would grant you, according to the riches of his glory, to **_be strengthened_** with might by his Spirit in the inner man;

Psalm 28:8 **_The LORD is their strength_**, and he is the saving strength of his anointed.

Psalm 29:11 **_The LORD gives His people strength_**; the LORD blesses His people with peace.

Psalm 119:28 My soul melts away for sorrow; **_strengthen me according to your word_**!

Nehemiah 8:10 ...Don't be dejected and sad, for the **_joy of the LORD is your strength_**!"

Joel 3:10 Beat your plowshares into swords And your pruning hooks into spears; **_Let the weak say, 'I am strong_**.'

Not one verse says, *"trials make you strong or grow you spiritually"*. Let's stick with the Word and Be Strong!

Now, let us dig a little deeper! Doc Murphy

CHAPTER ONE

REASONS WE GO THROUGH HARDSHIP

2 Timothy 2:3

King James Version Thou, therefore, **_endure hardness as a good soldier of Jesus Christ._**

Darby Bible Translation Take thy **_share in suffering_** as a good soldier of Jesus Christ.

World English Bible You, therefore, must endure hardship as a good soldier of Christ Jesus.

Young's Literal Translation thou, therefore**_, suffer evil_** as a good soldier of Jesus Christ;

Hardship, suffering evil, persecution, or trials are a part of the Christian walk. We are soldiers in the army of the Lord. There is spiritual warfare going on. In war, people suffer, but the suffering comes from the other side. As believers, **we train in the Word and prayer**. The actual suffering or hardship is coming from the adversary (the kingdom of darkness). Because we have adequately prepared, we know how to resist, counterattack, and attack the enemy. **_Yes, we experience hardship or suffering, but it is FOR Christ, not FROM Christ._**

*Phil 1:29 For to you it has been granted for Christ's sake, not only to believe in Him **but also to suffer <u>for His sake,</u>***

*Acts 5:41 And they departed from the presence of the council, **<u>rejoicing that they were counted worthy to suffer shame for his name.</u>***

*Romans 5:3 And not only so, **<u>but we glory in tribulations</u>** also: knowing that tribulation worketh patience;*

Paul said we glory IN tribulations, NOT FOR them. In other words, He wasn't saying we praise God FOR problems (as if God sent them), no, we praise God IN tribulation. **<u>We know</u>** we are overcomers through His grace!

*2 Corinthians 12:7 **<u>And lest I should be exalted above measure through the abundance of the revelations, there was given to me a thorn in the flesh, the messenger of Satan to buffet m</u>**e, lest I should be exalted above measure.*

The apostle Paul received great revelations from God, and the Devil didn't like it. He didn't want Paul to be exalted. To keep Paul down, SATAN (not God) influenced people (a thorn or persecution) to buffet Paul. The word buffet means to beat. Paul was abused as a result of His revelations he received from God. He was given a thorn (hardship, trial, suffering) by the ***"messenger of Satan."***

17 | Strong in Trials and Tribulations

People say God sent the thorn to keep Paul from being prideful**. But God didn't send the thorn. God sent the grace *(2 Cor 12:9)*.**

The words *"exalted above measure"* are taken from the Greek word **huperairo**, a compound of the words huper and airo. It means over, above, first-rate, first-class, top-notch, **Raise to the highest position.** The *Ambassador status means of the Highest Rank.* **Paul was an ambassador**. 2 Cor 5:20.

Satan sent the thorn. In knowing that Satan sent the thorn, we must ask the question: Why would Satan want to keep Paul from being prideful? Pride is one of his greatest tools. Well, we know Satan wasn't trying to keep Paul humble. That would be a Godly act. Only God wants us humble, *and He told us to humble ourselves (1 Peter 5:6).* Satan wants us puffed up. Satan is evil and would love for any of us to get puffed up or prideful. So we KNOW that Paul wasn't saying, *"God is doing this to me to keep me humble."*

Since the thorn came from Satan, this means Satan wasn't trying to humble Paul, but he was trying to keep Paul from being "exalted" to a place where the revelations would get out to the masses. Thus, **Satan was trying to kill Paul.**

When was Paul beaten?

Acts 14:19 And there came thither certain Jews from Antioch and Iconium, who persuaded the people, and, having stoned Paul, drew him out of the city, supposing he had been dead.

Paul was beaten with stones to the point that they thought he was dead. This was a thorn. This was the "messenger of Satan," trying to stop him. God didn't have anything to do with it. Paul endured. Paul succeeded with his faith, and the GRACE of God helped him.

2 Corinthians 12: 8 Three times, I pleaded with the Lord to take it away from me. **9** <u>But He said to me, "My grace is sufficient for you, for My power is perfected in weakness." Therefore I will boast all the more gladly in my weaknesses, so that the power of Christ may rest on me.</u> **10**That is why, for the sake of Christ, ***I delight in weaknesses, in insults, in hardships, in persecutions, in difficulties. For when I am weak, then I am strong.***

God's grace (empowerment) helped Paul. Paul rejoiced IN moments of physical weakness, not FOR weaknesses. God didn't give Paul the hardships or trials. God gave Paul GRACE to endure. God's grace made Paul strong to overcome. ***<u>The problems didn't make him strong. The grace did!</u>***

(Note: Read more about Paul's thorn in the Appendix)

2 Timothy 2:1 <u>New Living Translation</u> Timothy, my dear son, be strong through the grace that God gives you in Christ Jesus.

Paul's Testimony

2 Corinthians 4:8 *We are* hard-pressed on every side, **<u>*yet not crushed*</u>**; *we are* perplexed, **<u>*but not in despair;*</u>** [9] persecuted**<u>*, but not forsaken*</u>**; struck down, **<u>*but not destroyed*</u>**— [10] always carrying about in the body the dying of the Lord Jesus, that the life of Jesus also may be manifested in our body. [11] For we who live are always delivered to death for Jesus' sake, that the life of Jesus also may be manifested in our mortal flesh.

This is a man of faith. Paul is sharing with us that the thorn is terrible. Satan was trying to destroy him, but it didn't work. He has confidence, patience, and grace working. Trials were happening to him, but he was not destroyed or crushed.

When Satan sends thorns (hardship, suffering, pain, trials, testing, tribulation, affliction) your way, you rely on God's grace. Take His power and defeat the adversary. Yes, things will happen to you, but you must keep your faith and let patience work. You'll never do it if you think God is the one sending the hardship to you.

Folks, because of what God has placed in you (like He did Paul), Satan will send the thorn to try to stop you. Satan doesn't want your purpose revealed or in operation on this earth. He doesn't want you to do your assignment. He sends trials to keep you under. But you have to refuse to allow it to stop you. Press forward, rejoice, and resist the enemy!

Matthew 5:11 Blessed are you **when people insult you, persecute you**, and falsely say all kinds of evil against you **because of Me**. **12 Rejoice and be glad, because great is your reward in Heaven;** for in the same way they persecuted the prophets before you.

Jesus said we are blessed **when people** (NOT HIM) **persecute us.** We suffer persecution from people or the Devil because the Devil hates Jesus. We are on the same team as Jesus. Therefore, they hate us. The lies, hardship, persecution, or suffering doesn't come from Jesus. Tribulation comes because we are TEAM JESUS!

John 15:18 **"If the world hates you, keep in mind that it hated me first. ¹⁹ If you belonged to the world, it would love you as its own.** *As it is, you do not belong to the world, but I have chosen you out of the world. That is why the world hates you.*

Look at what God says:

Is 54:15 **_If anyone does attack you, it will not be my doing_**; whoever attacks you will surrender to you.

When most people go through hardship, they immediately think God is teaching them a lesson or maybe trying to get their attention. So they use the phrase, *"Everything happens for a reason,"* as if God and some kind of plan He has is THE REASON for their hardship. They get deceived with cute quotes like *"There is purpose in your pain."* Folks, the only purpose for pain is pain! God delivers **His people** from pain, not put them in pain. God gives everyone purpose by **telling** them what it is, not by giving pain.

Satan gives you pain to try to limit or destroy you! God can talk. He talks to His creation. Just listen to Him. Great teachers know how to teach you into purpose, not pain you into it. The Holy Spirit is a TEACHER. He is the TEACHER of the CHURCH (1 John 2:27). Bad life experiences are not your teacher. You grow spiritually by THE WORD OF GOD, not the WORLD OF SATAN (1 Peter 2:2).

If you're in the school of hard knocks, you either put yourself there or some pandemic happened that came from the works of darkness. God didn't. You can learn God's ways by listening, paying attention, studying, praying, and becoming intimate with the Father. No pain necessary. Yes, God disciplines those whom He loves, but that's still your fault (Heb 12:8-10). The Father of Spirits is not punishing a person doing what's right. God uses His Word to discipline us. It doesn't feel good at the time because it's a stiff rebuke, but He does it because He loves us. Once again, that is still your fault. God doesn't spank just for the heck of it.

God helps us

2 Corinthians 12:9 (NLT) The temptations in your life are no different from what others experience. And God is faithful. **He will not allow the temptation to be more than you can stand.** *When you are tempted,* **he will show you a way out** *so that you can endure.*

The Scripture _doesn't_ say, "God won't put more on you than you can bear." People have been saying this for centuries! God helps us escape. He is showing us a way out. He won't allow Satan to do more than we can stand. In other words, God is helping us (His people). He is not putting it on us! The Holy Spirit and Jesus are called the Helper or the Advocate *(1 John 2:1 and John 14:26)*. God is a helper of His people.

Ps 121:2 **My help comes from the LORD**, the Maker of Heaven and earth.

Jesus was led into the wilderness

23 | Strong in Trials and Tribulations

Matthew 4:1 Then Jesus was led by the Spirit into the wilderness to be **_tempted by the Devil_**. ² After fasting forty days and forty nights, he was hungry. ³ **_The tempter_** came to him and said, "If you are the Son of God, tell these stones to become bread." ⁴ Jesus answered, "It is written: 'Man shall not live on bread alone, but on every word that comes from the mouth of God.'" ⁵ Then the Devil took him to the holy city and had him stand on the highest point of the temple. ⁶ "If you are the Son of God," he said, "throw yourself down. For it is written: " 'He will command his angels concerning you, and they will lift you up in their hands so that you will not strike your foot against a stone.' [c]" ⁷ Jesus answered him, "It is also written: 'Do not put the Lord your God to the **test**.' " ⁸ Again, the Devil took him to a very high mountain and showed him all the kingdoms of the world and their splendor. ⁹ "All this I will give you," he said, "if you will bow down and worship me." ¹⁰ Jesus said to him**, "Away from me, Satan!** For it is written: 'Worship the Lord your God, and serve him only.' [e]" ¹¹ **Then the Devil left him,** and angels came and attended him.

Jesus is in the wilderness being tested by the Devil. Once again, God didn't test or tempt Jesus. The Devil did. Did you notice Satan is called "the Tempter"? You can also say, "The Tester." Jesus shows us how to win or succeed in trials (testing or temptation). Jesus had faith and patience because He stayed consistent in quoting Scripture every time the Devil tested Him. His faith was tested by the Devil, but He came out without a scratch because He endured until the end. Satan left Jesus for a season.

If we do the same thing Jesus did during moments of trials, we will come out on top every time, and Satan will flee from us as he did Jesus. What Jesus did was called "resisting the devil." We have the same authority and power. We just need to use it.

- **James 4:7** ⁷Submit yourselves, then, to God. **Resist the Devil, and he will flee** from you.

- Luke 10:19 Behold, **I have given you authority** to tread upon serpents and scorpions, and ***over all the power of the enemy: and nothing shall in any wise hurt you.***

There are two MAIN reasons why people go through hardship.

Reason #1 You made bad decisions, didn't listen to wise counsel, and now you're going through hardship as a result of your lack of wisdom. Read this story in Acts 27:

Acts 27: ⁹ Much time had been lost, and sailing had already become dangerous because by now it was after the Day of Atonement. **So Paul warned**

25 | Strong in Trials and Tribulations

them,* ¹⁰ *"Men, I can see that our voyage is going to be disastrous and bring great loss to ship and cargo, and to our own lives also." ¹¹ But the centurion, instead of listening to what Paul said, followed the advice of the pilot and of the owner of the ship *...* ¹⁸ ***We took such a violent battering from the storm*** *that the next day they began to throw the cargo overboard.* ¹⁹ *On the third day, they threw the ship's tackle overboard with their own hands.* ²⁰ ***When neither sun nor stars appeared for many days and the storm continued raging, we finally gave up all hope of being saved.*** ²¹ *After they had gone a long time without food,* ***Paul stood up before them and said: "Men, you should have taken my advice not to sail from Crete; then you would have spared yourselves this damage and loss***. ²² *But now I urge you to keep up your courage because not one of you will be lost; only the ship will be destroyed.* ²³ *Last night an angel of the God to whom I belong and whom I serve stood beside me* ²⁴ *and said, 'Do not be afraid, Paul. You must stand trial before Caesar, and God has graciously given you the lives of all who sail with you.'* ²⁵ *So keep up your courage, men, for I have faith in God that it will happen just as he told me.*

Why did they suffer hardship? Why were they in tribulation? Answer: THEY DIDN'T LISTEN TO THE ADVICE OF THE WISE MAN (PAUL). They made the wrong decision. Not listening to wise counsel, doing your own thing, making decisions that don't line up with wisdom will put you right into unnecessary storms, suffering, hardship, trials, and tribulations. God didn't do it, and in this case, neither did the Devil.

- *Proverbs 12:15 Fools **think their own way is right**, but the **wise listen to others**.*

Be wise and listen when your spiritual leaders are speaking wisdom to you. Especially listen when you're about to make a significant decision.

Notice the love and grace of God in that story. They put themselves in a bad situation, and God still helped them. Not one person was destroyed. God's heart is to help, not destroy. Even while you're destroying YOUR OWN life, God will have mercy.

Reason #2 The Devil is trying to destroy your life! Jesus, the apostles, the saints all went through persecution, hardship, tribulation, trials, suffering, and it came from the Devil. In the case of everyone else outside of Jesus, some of it was a result of disobedience, lack of wisdom, making wrong decisions, and sin. The good news is you can still be strong and overcome using the power and wisdom of God! JUST STOP BLAMING IT ON GOD!

1 Peter 5: [8] Be sober, be vigilant; because your **adversary the Devil,** as a roaring lion, walketh about, **seeking whom he may devour:**

CHAPTER TWO

MAXIMUM JOY!

At all times and at any given time *(except for tragedies)* Christians should be the happiest people alive.

"Joy is a spiritual force and a demonstration of the triumph of Christ" – Mark Hankins

James 1:2-4 NKJV My brethren, ***count it all joy when you fall into various trials***, knowing that the testing of your faith produces patience. But let patience have its perfect work, that you may be perfect and complete, lacking nothing.

<u>New International Version</u>
Consider it pure joy, my brothers and sisters, whenever you face trials of many kinds,

<u>New Living Translation</u>
Dear brothers and sisters, when troubles of any kind come your way, ***consider it an opportunity for great joy***.

(Berkeley) ***Consider it maximum joy...***

Joy: delight, exhilaration, rejoicing, glee, gladness

Maximum: the greatest or highest amount possible, extreme.

As we can see, the Apostle James [by the Holy Spirit] is telling us to have **MAXIMUM JOY** during times of trials. We are to count it as an **opportunity for great joy**. **Extreme praise** should be going on! When you go through tribulation that's your opportunity to have **GREAT JOY**, not great sadness!

We are accustomed to getting happy when things are going well but we must get accustomed to living like where we really are which is the Kingdom of God. In this Kingdom, **we get happy when things are going bad**. We have a supernatural joy that's hard to explain to the world. You didn't even get this joy from the world.

1 Peter 4:16 But it is no shame to suffer for being a Christian. ***Praise God for the privilege*** of being called by his name!

In our society, it's popular to NOT be okay and that has become okay. It's popular to always talk about problems that have no solutions. It's popular to be down all the time and get people to feel sorry for you. **It's more popular to be sad, not okay, gloomy, frustrated, depressed, and negative than it is to be full of faith, victorious, and full of joy. But we are changing that, and, in our churches, we are normalizing joy and victory.**

Strong in Trials and Tribulations

James says, *"Count it ALL joy when you go through trials"*. Whatever evil test comes to you **from the devil** you should count it all joy. The victory that comes with the Holy Spirit gives you joy during storms. You start counting it maximum joy!

If you have 10 problems, then you have 10 opportunities to rejoice. Count it all joy!

- ***1 Peter 1:6-8 Wherein ye greatly rejoice***, *though now for a season, if need be, ye are in heaviness through manifold temptations: …*

- ***1 Peter 1:6*** *In this you greatly rejoice, though now for a little while you may have had to suffer grief in various trials.*

Our response to trouble is JOY! Our response to difficulties is joy. We cheer up when we go through storms because we believe God.

Why can you have maximum joy?

2 Peter 2:9 *The Lord knoweth how to deliver the godly out of temptations,* and to reserve the unjust unto the day of judgment to be punished:

James 1:12 Blessed *is* the man that endureth temptation: for when he is tried, ***he shall receive the***

crown of life, which the Lord hath promised to them that love him.

Blessed should be translated HAPPY.

Ps 34:19 The righteous person may have many troubles, ***but the LORD delivers him from them all***;

Matthew 5:12 ***Rejoice and be glad***, because ***great is your reward in heaven***; for in the same way they persecuted the prophets before you.

You can have maximum joy because God is a Deliverer. If you believe that, then you should have joy and that joy forces you to react with praise.

Many people don't have joy because they are not filled with the Holy Ghost!

- Romans 14:17 NLT "For the Kingdom of God is not a matter of what we eat or drink, but of living a life of goodness and peace ***and joy in the Holy Spirit.***"

- Eph 5:18 Do not get drunk on wine, which leads to reckless indiscretion. ***Instead, be filled with the Spirit.*** 19 Speak to one another with psalms, hymns, and spiritual songs. ***Sing and make music in your hearts*** to the Lord,

The Holy Ghost gives you joy and empowers you to rejoice and be happy at the most unusual times.

The Fruit of the Spirit or the DNA of God; the character of God is on the inside of the Believer. **You have JOY**, but you must exercise it. It is not a fake joy. It is the real deal. You have real joy; therefore, your praise and rejoicing should be real. You don't have to fake it until you make it. No, there is real joy inside of you. So, you can REALly rejoice during trials and hardship. *Gal 5:22*

Eph 3:16 I pray that out of his glorious riches he may strengthen you with power through his Spirit in your inner being,

You are strengthened in your inner man with mighty power by the Holy Ghost, but the joy of the Lord is your strength. Where do you get the joy?

Nehemiah 8:10 "Do not grieve, for <u>the joy of the Lord is your strength.</u>"

Hab 3:17 Though the fig tree should not blossom,
nor fruit be on the vines,
the produce of the olive fail
and the fields yield no food,
the flock be cut off from the fold
and there be no herd in the stalls,
¹⁸ <u>*yet I will rejoice in the LORD;*</u>
<u>*I will take joy in the God of my salvation.*</u>

¹⁹ GOD, **_the Lord, is my strength;_**
he makes my feet like the deer's;
he makes me tread on my high places.

Joy is having a serious attitude change.

*Attitude: **a settled way of thinking or feeling** about someone or something, typically one that is reflected in a person's behavior. A frame of mind, stance.*

What is your attitude?

Everything can be taken from a man but one thing: the last of the human freedoms—to choose one's attitude in any given set of circumstances, to choose one's own way. Viktor Frankl

"Frankl is perhaps most famous for surviving the Holocaust. In 1942 Frankl and his family were sent to the Theresienstadt camp. Here his father died, and in 1944 Frankl and his remaining family were moved to Auschwitz where his mother was killed, his wife died shortly after.

In 1945, after the liberation of camps by Allied forces, Frankl returned to his home city of Vienna where he wrote the book Man's Search For Meaning, in which he detailed the life in the camps, the brutality and destitution of the conditions, and the fall into despair and hopelessness of his fellow prisoners."

Viktor sounds like he learned and understood contentment. When you learn contentment, you will have joy.

In any and all circumstances I have learned the secret [of being content] - *whether well-fed or hungry, whether in abundance or in need. I am able to do all things through Him who strengthens me" (Phil. 4:12-13)*

Contentment: a state of happiness and satisfaction.

"Contentment is an emotional state of satisfaction that can be seen as a mental state drawn from being at ease in one's situation, body, and mind".

Contentment does not mean you have settled into a bad situation believing it will always be that way. No, you are happy and full of joy because you're walking by faith, you're patient, you can suffer long, you have self-control, and you know that God will deliver you!

What God says brings joy

Instead of getting sad over what the devil said, go ahead and get happy over what God said.

Ps 119:162 **_I rejoice in your word_** like one who discovers a great treasure.

Ps 119:162 **_I'm ecstatic over what you say_**, like one who strikes it rich.

Your celebration is a demonstration of your expectation of what God said. – Mark Hankins and Doc Murphy (I added the "of what God said"…haha)

When you're expecting what God said to manifest you will have joy. Sad, being down, slipping slowly into madness, gloomy, worried, and fear are not signs of expectation. They are signs that you don't believe or expect God's Word to be true.

Joy is the bridge between believing and receiving. (1 Peter 1:8-9).

Ps 119:114 <u>Contemporary English Version</u>
<u>Obeying your instructions brings as much happiness</u> as being rich.

<u>English Revised Version</u>
I have rejoiced in the way of thy testimonies, as much as in all riches.

<u>GOD'S WORD® Translation</u>
I find joy in the way [shown by] your written instructions more than I find joy in all kinds of riches.

- **_<u>Psalm 1:2</u> But his delight is in the Law of the LORD_**, *and on His law he meditates day and night.*

- ***Psalm 19:8** The precepts of the LORD are right, bringing joy to the heart; the commandments of the LORD are radiant, giving light to the eyes.*

- ***Psalm 112:1** Hallelujah! Blessed is the man who fears the LORD, who greatly delights in His commandments.*

- ***Psalm 119:111** Your testimonies are my heritage forever, for they are the joy of my heart.*

The more you honor and rejoice at His Word and obey it, the more you will have joy in your life. Depression is defeated.

Don't let the devil tell you it's just normal to be sad and react that way when things don't go your way. No, you should normalize joy. Normalize praise. Normalize victory. We walk by faith and not by sight or feelings! Forget the agenda of a weak and defeated society and weak Christians who want to stay weak. Stick with the Bible and the lifestyle of Kingdom Citizens.

CHAPTER THREE

LET PATIENCE WORK

James 1:2 (Complete Jewish Bible) **Regard it all as joy**, *my brothers when you* **face various kinds of temptations**; *³ for you know that the* **testing of your trust** *produces perseverance. ⁴ But let perseverance do its complete work; so that you may be complete and whole, lacking in nothing.*

When we face trials, testing, or temptations, we are to have joy. Why? We know that when we succeed in overcoming them, we develop. The tests don't *come* to develop us. They come to destroy us. It's when we succeed or overcome the testing is when we build endurance.

James 1:3 **Good News Translation** *for you know that* **when your faith succeeds in facing such trials**, *the result is the ability to endure.*

As you can see, James is not saying the test comes to grow you. No, you succeed by using your faith. Your faith is what causes you to grow in endurance.

There are many people facing trials, **and they never succeed, develop, or grow**. They have the mindset to stay in the test so they can grow or get strong. This kind of thinking has caused many to lose out in life. They live defeated lives. They never use their faith to come out of testing. It's hard to use your faith when you think God is the One testing or tempting you.

James 1:12 How blessed is the man who **perseveres through temptation!** For after he has **passed the test** (not failed the test), he will receive as his crown the Life which God has promised to those who love him. **¹³ No one being tempted should say, "I am being tempted by God." For God cannot be tempted by evil, and God himself tempts no one.**

James 1:12 (AMP) Blessed (happy, to be envied) is the man *who is patient under trial and stands up (not sit down and take it) under temptation*, for when he has stood the test *and* been approved, he will receive [the victor's] crown of life which God has promised to those who love Him. **¹³ Let no one say when he is tempted, I am tempted from God; for God is incapable of being tempted by [what is] evil and He Himself tempts no one.**

Notice the words temptation, testing, and trial are used interchangeably. They mean the same thing. As you can see, we are to be patient when facing difficulties. We are to STAND UP, not sit down and take it. Faith overcomes the world. When we go through trials, we employ or hire patience. This doesn't mean we put up with the test. It means that when our faith or our belief system is tested, *we stay consistent* in what we believe no matter what is going on. We know that God is our Redeemer,

Deliverer, Savior, Blesser, Healer, Source, Provider, Waymaker, Faithful King, Wonderful Counselor, and Mighty God! We know, and we stand firm on our belief when facing temptation (test or trials). Patience undergirds my faith. It helps me to remain consistent in my confession of faith, and it helps me to endure until the end.

Matthew 10:22 You will be hated by everyone on account of My name**, *but the one who perseveres to the end will be saved.***

Luke 21:19 By ***your patient endurance***, you will gain your souls.

Faith and Patience

Hebrews 6:12 *We do not want you to become lazy, but to imitate those who* **through faith and patience inherit** *what has been promised.*

Faith and patience work together. Patience helps your faith to endure. While you're trusting God, it is patience that causes you to be consistent in your trust even when storms are raging. This is how you inherit what you believe God for. You can have faith, but if you don't have patience, then you will not get to the end of your faith. Your faith is going to be tested. But patience helps you succeed in overcoming the test, trials, tribulations, or temptations.

Don't imitate or follow those who through "doubt and impatience," try to get something from God. It doesn't work. Those shouldn't be your mentors. Follow those who truly believe God and are patient until they reach the end. These people are developed, mature, and faithful to God and His Word.

1 Peter 1:8 **Though you have not seen Him**, you love Him; and though you do not see Him now, **you believe** in Him and rejoice with an inexpressible and glorious joy**, 9 receiving the end of your faith**—the salvation of *your* souls.

This Scripture is talking about believing what (or whom) you can't see, and at the end of that, you receive the salvation of your souls. But there is a principle here: You believe what you can't see, then you receive. Believing takes you to the end of your faith. In other words, you get the result of what you believed God for. But to get to the end, you are going to have to work patience or let patience have her perfect work in you.

*Romans 15:4 For whatsoever things were written aforetime were written for our learning**, that we through patience and comfort of the scriptures might have hope.***

Notice, through **patience** and the **comfort of Scriptures,** we have hope. It **didn't say**, *"through hardship,* we have hope".

CHAPTER FOUR

THE JOB SYNDROME

Job 2:7 So Satan (not God) went out from the presence of the LORD and afflicted Job…

Job 42:3 You asked, 'Who is this that obscures my plans without knowledge?' Surely, I spoke of things I did not understand, things too wonderful for me to know.

Job 42:6 I take back everything I said, and I sit in dust and ashes to show my repentance.

Job's story has confused many. Many verses in the Old testament have confused many concerning the nature of God. If you want to know the true nature of God, LOOK TO JESUS. You will NEVER see Jesus describing Himself the way Old Testament characters did. Just because they said it doesn't mean it was true. Job said the Lord gives, and the Lord takes away (Job 1:21). Job said the Lord slew him (Job 13:15). He didn't realize it was **_the Devil who did the "slaying" and the "taking away."_** Job told his wife in Job 2:10 that they should accept good and trouble from God. That sounds noble and humble, but it was not valid. Job didn't know that Satan troubled him. The Devil has been trying to get God to work evil against His obedient children for thousands of years. Satan told God to afflict Job, but God wouldn't do it.

Strong in Trials and Tribulations

Job 2:3 And he still maintains his integrity, ***though you incited me against him to ruin him without any reason."*** ⁴ "Skin for skin!" Satan replied. "A man will give all he has for his own life. ⁵ ***But now stretch out your hand and strike his flesh and bones, and he will surely curse you to your face."***
⁶ The LORD said to Satan, "Very well, then, ***he is in your hands;*** but you must spare his life."

Satan tried twice to get God to destroy Job's life. It's not in God's nature to do that. God would not and could not do it.

Side note: Even the people whom God has given and will give righteous judgment to in the end, it was and is because of their wickedness. It's not His nature to destroy people, but it is His nature to give righteous judgment to the wicked and those who disobey.

Look at what Jesus (God manifested in the flesh) told His apostles:

Luke 9: ⁵² And sent messengers before his face: and they went, and entered into a village of the Samaritans, to make ready for him. ⁵³ ***And they did not receive him,*** because his face was as though he would go to Jerusalem. ⁵⁴ And when his disciples James and John saw this**, *they said, Lord, wilt thou that we command fire to come down from Heaven***, and consume them, even as Elias did? ⁵⁵ **But he turned, and rebuked them, and said, Ye know not what manner of spirit ye are of.** ⁵⁶ **For the Son of**

man is not come to destroy men's lives, but to save them. And they went to another village.

Jesus (God with us, Mighty God, Everlasting Father) said He came to save men, not to destroy them. Jesus is the full expression (glory) manifestation or nature of God. God didn't change and hasn't changed. Jesus told his apostles that they were of another spirit. This means the spirit of the Devil.

Why was Satan permitted *(in the sense that God didn't stop it)* to do things to Job? Answer: Satan is the *God of this world* and *the prince of the power of the air*. Job was also full of fear.

- 2 Corinthians 4:4 *In whom* **the God of this world** *hath blinded the minds of them which believe not, lest the light of the glorious gospel of Christ, who is the image of God, should shine unto them.*
- *Ephesians 2:1 As for you, you were dead in your trespasses and sins, 2 in which you used to walk when you conformed to the ways of this world and of the* **prince of the power of the air, the spirit who is now at work in the sons of disobedience.**

Notice Satan's spirit works in the sons of DISobedience. Which means it's not God's Spirit.

Satan was kicked out of Heaven to the earth. This is his domain. He has the right to do evil here. But this is why we must understand our authority. **We have the right to stop the Devil.** Jesus showed us this.

"Satan has the right to work evil. We have the right to stop Satan's wickedness".

Luke 10:17 The seventy-two returned with joy and said, "Lord, **_even the demons submit to us in Your name._**" 18 **_So He said to them, "I saw Satan fall like lightning from Heaven._** 19 **_See, I have given you authority_** to tread on snakes and scorpions, and over all the power of the enemy. Nothing will harm you

Side Note: Jesus saw Satan fall. Satan fell before Jesus was born. How did Jesus see it? Correct! HE IS GOD

Is 14:12 *How are you fallen from Heaven, O Lucifer, son of the morning! How are you cut down to the ground, which did weaken the nations!*

Satan has been causing havoc and weakening nations from the beginning.

By the way, the Jews knew that only God had the authority to cast out demons, raise the dead, and heal the sick. This is why they were confused about Jesus. Not only did Jesus do it, but He also gave others authority and power to do it as He did. The Jews who didn't believe called it blasphemy and tried to kill Him. They didn't realize that Jesus was the Messiah or God manifested in the flesh.

- *Mark 11:28 After their return to Jerusalem, Jesus was walking in the temple courts, and the chief priests, scribes, and elders came up to Him.* **28 "By what authority are You doing these things?"** *they asked. "And who gave You the authority to do t hem?"*
- *John 14:12 Verily, verily, I say unto you, He that believeth on me,* **the works that I do shall he also do;** *and greater works than these shall he do; because I go unto my Father.*

The Old Testament Saints didn't have the Holy Spirit in them and the power and authority that the New Covenant Believers have. Many believers are still trying to live like Old Testament Saints instead of New Testament Saints. You will not see the kind of language that you read in the Old Testament in the New Testament.

Jesus didn't put sickness on people, and He didn't do it ***JUST*** to heal them! That's ridiculous and **_unnecessary_**. Jesus didn't cause Lazarus' illness.

John 11:4 So the sisters sent word to Jesus, "Lord, the one You love is sick." 4 When Jesus heard this, He said, _"This sickness will not end in death._ No, it is for the glory of God, so that the Son of God may be glorified through it."

45 | Strong in Trials and Tribulations

The "sickness" was not for God's glory. Jesus raising Lazarus up was for God's glory.

Jesus knew He would raise Lazarus from the dead, and He did it (RAISING HIM UP) for a sign for unbelievers. The Lazarus story is not something we are supposed to preach as a rule and as a way to say, *"God is allowing bad things to happen to you as a setup."* This was an exception to get people to believe. It was merely a sign.

*John 11:14 So then he told them plainly, "Lazarus is dead, [15] and **for your sake, I am glad I was not there, so that you may believe. Verse 40** Then Jesus said, "Did I not tell you that if you believe, you will see the glory of God?" [41] So they took away the stone. Then Jesus looked up and said, "Father, I thank you that you have heard me. [42] I knew that you always hear me, **but I said this for the benefit of the people standing here, that they may believe that you sent me.**" [43] When he had said this, Jesus called in a loud voice, "Lazarus, come out!" [44] The dead man came out, his hands and feet wrapped with strips of linen and a cloth around his face. Jesus said to them, "Take off the grave clothes and let him go."*

The sickness and death came from the Devil. **The healing and resurrection came from God-Jesus

- *Hebrews 2:14 Now since the children have flesh and blood, He too shared in their humanity, so that by His death **He might destroy him who holds the power of death,***

that is, the Devil,
- ***John 11:25*** *Jesus said to her, "I am the resurrection and the life. He who believes in Me, though he may die, he shall live.* ^{26} *And whoever lives and believes in Me shall never die. Do you believe this?*
- Acts 10:38 How God anointed **Jesus** of Nazareth with the Holy Ghost and with power: **who went about doing good and healing all** that **were oppressed of the Devil,** for God was with him.

Satan is behind sickness and disease (trials, evil, and testings). You can't have faith for healing or anything if you don't know what God's will is or know the nature of God and the nature of the Devil. If you think God is doing what Satan is doing, you'll never have faith in God's love to work in your life.

"Love is the producer of miracles, not the producer of pain."

The New Testament Believer is under grace through faith. *We operate on the lane of grace, and faith is the vehicle to get us to our destination*. The authority given to us puts us in a position to act like God here on the earth the SAME way Jesus did. If there were problems, you NEVER saw Jesus (the son of man) blaming God. No, He blamed the Devil and He never said God allowed it. He used His authority and defeated the Devil. ***Jesus never said God heals and harms.***

*Luke 13:16 Then should not this woman, a daughter of Abraham, **whom Satan has kept bound for eighteen long years**, be set free on the Sabbath day from what bound her?"*

Who had the woman bound for 18 years? Correct, SATAN. God didn't allow it for 18 years. When someone came who understood authority and how to use power, that person (Jesus) set the woman free from what SATAN did to her.

*Luke 13:10 On a Sabbath, Jesus was teaching in one of the synagogues, ¹¹ and a woman was there who had been **crippled by a spirit** for eighteen years. She was bent over and could not straighten up at all. ¹² When Jesus saw her, **he called her forward and said to her, "Woman, you are set free from your infirmity." ¹³ Then he put his hands on her, and immediately she straightened up and praised God.***

The woman was crippled by a spirit (Not God's spirit. The spirit of the Devil). Jesus healed her. He didn't say this pain is for a purpose. No, He simply healed her *from* the pain. He didn't heal her *in* the pain.

Jesus took care of IT

If Jesus healed or cured people of IT, preached against IT, or cast IT out, then understand that He didn't put IT on them. He didn't put them through IT. Neither did He allow IT.

- Acts 10:38 And you know that God anointed Jesus of Nazareth with the Holy Spirit and with power. Then Jesus went around doing good and healing all who were oppressed by the Devil, for God was with him.
- Matthew 4:23 Jesus went throughout Galilee, teaching in their synagogues, preaching the gospel of the kingdom, and healing every disease and sickness among the people.
- 1 John 4:18 There is no fear in love, but perfect love casts out fear. For fear has to do with punishment, and whoever fears has not been perfected in love.
- Matthew 4:24 News about Him spread all over Syria, and people brought to Him all who were ill with various diseases, those suffering acute pain, the demon-possessed, those having seizures, and the paralyzed--and He healed them.
- John 1:29 The next day, John saw Jesus coming toward him and said, "Look, the Lamb of God, who takes away the sin of the world!

God equipped you to handle the Devil. And if you need equipment, just ASK!

Ephesians 6:10 Finally, be strong in the Lord and in his mighty power. 11 Put on the full armor of God, so that you can take your stand against the Devil's schemes. ⁱ² For our struggle is not against flesh and blood, but against the rulers, against the authorities, against the powers of this dark world and against the spiritual forces of evil in the heavenly realms. ¹³ Therefore put on the full armor of God, so that when the day of evil comes, you may be able to stand your ground, and after you have done everything, to stand. ¹⁴ Stand firm then, with the belt of truth buckled around your waist, with the breastplate of righteousness in place, ¹⁵ and with your feet fitted with the readiness that comes from the gospel of peace. ¹⁶ In addition to all this, take up the shield of faith, with which you can extinguish all the flaming arrows of the evil one. ¹⁷ Take the helmet of salvation and the sword of the Spirit, which is the word of God. ¹⁸ And pray in the Spirit on all occasions with all kinds of prayers and requests. With this in mind, be alert and always keep on praying for all the Lord's people.

Let's break down a few points in Ephesians 6:

1. We are responsible for being STRONG, not weak.

2. We have equipment called the ***"Armor of God,"*** and <u>***we are responsible for putting it on***</u>. No wonder so many are defeated- they don't have their armor on. We think God is going to do everything He told us to do, so we never bother with the armor.

3. We put on the Armor to take our STAND against the Devil's schemes or tricks. Notice God is not the blame. Paul said we are standing against the Devil.

4. Paul tells us who the struggle or the fight is against. Nowhere in there did He say, *"God is bringing on the struggle to make you stronger."* No, he said to be strong in the Lord because the struggle is against the Devil. The struggle doesn't make you strong. You're supposed to be already strong by drawing strength from God!! Trials, tribulations, tests, or struggles don't make you strong. They are designed to make you weak.

"God DIDN'T send the giants in your life. He sent His Word so you can whip the giants that the Devil sent."

God wants you strong so that you can defeat those things. **You get strong in the power of His might**. Read these verses:

- *Neh 8:10 Do not grieve, for the joy of the Lord is your strength.*

- *Eph 3:16 I pray that **out of his glorious riches he may strengthen you with power through his Spirit** in your inner being,*

- *Eph 6:10 Finally, be strong in the Lord and in His mighty power. 11Put on the full armor of God, so that you can make your stand against the Devil's schemes.*

- *Is 41:10 So do not fear, for I am with you; do not be dismayed, for I am your God. I will strengthen you and help you; I will uphold you with my righteous right hand.*
- *Is 40:30, But those who hope in the Lord will renew their strength. They will soar on wings like eagles; they will run and not grow weary, they will walk and not be faint.*
- *Ps 73:26 My flesh and my heart may fail, but God is the strength of my heart and my portion forever.*
- *Phil 4:13 I can do all this through him who gives me strength.*
- *Is 40:29 He gives strength to the weary and increases the power of the weak.*
- *Ps 18:1-2 I love you, Lord, my strength. The Lord is my rock, my fortress, and my deliverer; my God is my rock, in whom I take refuge, my shield, and the horn of my salvation, my stronghold.*
- *Hab 3:19 The Sovereign Lord is my strength; he makes my feet like the feet of a deer; he enables me to tread on the heights.*

The point is if you don't take the responsibility to put on the equipment and use it to fight and win against the enemy, you will be defeated, **and a defeated athlete usually blames the coach!**

Meditate these verses:

- *Luke 10:9 Behold, I give unto you power to tread on serpents and scorpions, and over all the power of the enemy: and nothing shall by any means hurt you.*
- *Matthew 10:10 And when he had called unto him his twelve disciples, he gave them power against unclean spirits, to cast them out, and to heal all manner of sickness and all manner of disease.*
- *James 1:5 If any of you lacks wisdom, you should ask God, who gives generously to all without finding fault, and it will be given to you.*
- *Matthew 7:7 <u>Ask, and it will be given to you; seek and you will find; knock, and the door will be opened to you.</u> 8 For everyone who asks receives; he who seeks finds; and to him who knocks, the door will be opened.*

CHAPTER FIVE

THE TRIAL OF YOUR FAITH

1 Peter 1:6 In this you greatly rejoice, though now for a little while **you may have had to suffer grief in various trials** 7 **so that the authenticity of your faith—** more precious than gold, which perishes even though refined by fire— **may result in praise, glory, and honor at the revelation of Jesus Christ.**

Any time someone goes on trial, it is the DA's office or prosecutor (accuser) that puts the person on trial. The defense attorney or advocate doesn't put anyone on trial; they defend the person who is on trial. The judge is the one who has the power and authority to make a judgment.

When we look at this from a spiritual perspective, we can see in Scripture, who is the prosecutor, the Judge, and the Advocate or Defense Attorney. God is the Judge. Satan is the *accuser of the brethren* or prosecutor (the one who tries people). Jesus/The Holy Spirit is the Advocate or Defense Attorney. Jesus is the Helper. The Holy Spirit is the Comforter, which is translated, Helper. The Holy Spirit is also called the Advocate. Jesus pleads our cause in front of the Judge. The accuser (Satan) accuses us or puts us on trial to try to secure a verdict of guilty. He also tries our faith hoping the trial would weaken us, cause us to quit, keep us from receiving from God and hopefully keep us from moving forward in the things of God.

- **1 John 2:1-5** ₁My dear children, I write this to you so that you will not sin. But if anybody does sin, we have an advocate with the Father-Jesus Christ, the Righteous One. ₂He is the atoning sacrifice for our sins, and not only for ours but also for the sins of the whole world.
- **John 14:26** ₂₆But the Advocate, **the Holy Spirit**, whom the Father will send in my name, will teach you all things and will remind you of everything I have said to you.
- **Isaiah 33:22 For the LORD is our Judge.** The LORD is our lawgiver. The LORD is our King. He will save us.
- James 4:12 **God alone, who gave the law, is the Judge.** He alone has the power to save or to destroy. So what right do you have to judge your neighbor?

(Note: God The Judge saves His people as long as they are obedient to His word. He has and will destroy the wicked. Get the point?)

- Revelation 12:9 And the great dragon was cast out, that old serpent, called the **_Devil, and Satan, which deceiveth the whole world: he was cast out_** into the earth, and his angels were cast out with him. ₁₀And I heard a loud voice saying in Heaven, Now is come salvation, and strength, and the kingdom of our God, and the power of his Christ: **_for the accuser of our brethren is cast down, which accused them before our God day and night._** ₁₁**_And they overcame him by the blood of the Lamb, and by the word of their testimony;_** they loved not their lives unto the death.

Satan is known as "the accuser of the brethren" (Revelation 12:10). He accuses us of our sins and shortcomings before God. He also makes up lies to try to get us in trouble with God. Satan doesn't want God to extend grace and forgiveness to us, nor does he want us to receive God's grace or receive anything from God. Jesus says of Satan, *"He was a murderer from the beginning, and does not stand in the truth, because there is no truth in him (John 8:44).*

I love watching court cases and crime shows. I've noticed that a lot of the convictions that the prosecutors obtain are a result of the many lies told and evidence that was held back. They do it just to secure a guilty verdict. Many of them are crooks and liars! Satan is the same. All he wants to do is put people on trial and lie. He is hoping to get a guilty verdict. He tried to kill Jesus, Paul, Peter, and all the Saints who were giving him trouble. When Satan tries you, stand up and use the armor of God, plead the blood of Jesus, and defeat the rascal!

During trials, we must hold fast to our confession of faith (Hebrews 10:23). We must stand firm. The heat will be turned up, but if you remain consistent in standing and refuse to waver, you will come out of those trials with praise, glory, and honor. **It's God's strength that keeps you strong during the trial.**

In the Old Covenant, you see David and others saying God tested them or tried them. He righteously tested them but not the way Satan does.
God tested *(proved to see what was in their hearts, not to destroy them)* Israel when He allowed *(didn't stop it)* them to go through the wilderness. By the way, the length of time they stayed and all the

foolishness they did was their fault, not God doing it to them. THEY sinned, complained, and disrespected leadership.

Deut 8:2 And thou shalt remember all the way which the LORD thy God led thee these forty years in the wilderness, to humble thee, |and| **to prove thee, to know what** |was| **in thine heart,** whether thou wouldest keep his commandments, or no.

God just wanted to see if they would trust Him for food and provision. He fed them, clothed them, gave them a leader, gave them a covenant, and more. THEY SINNED AND MESSED UP!

The reality is God didn't test them in an *evil way* like most think. **God tested Abraham but no harm came to Abraham or Isaac.**

Gen 22:1 *Later God tested Abraham* and called to him, "Abraham!" "Yes, here I am!" he answered. **2** God said, "Take your son, your only son Isaac, whom you love, and go to Moriah. Sacrifice him there as a burnt offering on one of the mountains that I will show you." **3** Early the next morning Abraham saddled his donkey. He took with him two of his servants and his son Isaac. When he had cut the wood for the burnt offering, he set out for the place that God had told him about. **4** Two days later Abraham saw the place in the distance. **5** Then Abraham said to his servants, "You stay here with the donkey while the boy and I go over there. We'll worship. After that we'll come back to you." **6** Then Abraham took the wood for the burnt offering and gave it to his son Isaac. Abraham carried the burning coals and the knife. The two of them went on together. **7** Isaac spoke up and said, "Father?" "Yes, Son?" Abraham answered. Isaac asked, "We have the burning coals and the wood, but where is the lamb for the burnt offering?" **8** Abraham answered, "God will provide a lamb for the burnt offering, Son." The two of them went on together. **9** When they came to the place that God had told him about, Abraham built the altar and arranged the wood on it. Then he tied up his son Isaac and laid him on top of the wood on the altar. **10** Next, Abraham picked up the knife and took it in his hand to sacrifice his son. **11** But the Messenger of the Lord called to him from heaven and said, "Abraham! Abraham!" "Yes?" he answered. *12 "Do not lay a hand on the boy," he said. "Do not do anything to him. Now I know that you fear God, because you did not refuse to give me your son, your only son."* **13** When Abraham looked around, he saw a ram behind him caught by its horns in a bush. So Abraham took the ram and sacrificed it as a burnt offering in place of his son. **14** Abraham named that place The Lord Will Provide. It is still said today, "On the mountain of the Lord it will be provided."

The test God gave Abraham was harmless, righteous, and full of love. Satan's tests are full of hate, harm, and destruction. See the difference? People mix up the testing of the Lord and the testing of the devil. Others were tested by God, but it was righteous testing not evil.

The words, test, trial, temptation, suffering, and so forth are all interchangeable words, and God clearly said He doesn't try (test) or ***tempt anyone with evil (sin)***, and He can't be tempted by evil. (James 1:13).

Job went through a major trial. It was Satan trying Job or testing Job. The three Hebrews boys were put in the fire by the King, not God. Daniel was thrown to the Lions by the King, not God. God saved him. God saved Shadrach, Meshach, and Abednego. He didn't do it to them. **He saved them FROM it.** God is the Savior of His people! That's His heart. That's His nature.

Psalm 37:39 *The salvation of the righteous is from the LORD; He is their stronghold in time of trouble.*

Psalm 37:40 *The LORD helps and delivers them; He rescues and saves them from the wicked because they take refuge in Him.*

Isaiah 41:10 *Do not fear, for I am with you; do not be afraid, for I am your God. I will strengthen you; I will surely help you; I will uphold you with My right hand of righteousness.*

So even though you go through the trials of the Devil as Joseph, Moses, Paul, Peter, David, the 3 Hebrew boys, and other Saints of God did, you will come out on top just as they did because God is your Savior, and your faith and trust are only in Him! STAND STRONG during TRIALS AND TRIBULATION!

I pray you were helped. Take the Scriptures laid out in this book and meditate them. It's the Word that will strengthen you, build your faith, and help you overcome every demonic trial and test. Be firm during the tribulation and think like an overcomer!

Be Blessed

Doc Murphy

About the Author

Pastor, author, songwriter/producer, and entrepreneur, Doc Murphy has been a transformative voice and leader for over three decades, impacting lives across the nation and around the world. As the visionary founder of The Everywhere Network and Doc Murphy Movements, he and his wife, Mary, have planted churches in multiple cities while also teaching and raising up leaders. Mary travels nationally as a recording artist, sharing the gospel through powerful worship experiences.

Doc has been featured on major networks such as TBN, CTC, and numerous other television and radio platforms. His interviews, teachings, and sermons have inspired and touched countless lives. He also hosts the global podcast "Kingdom Success Everywhere" on the Charisma Podcasting Network (CPN), equipping listeners with biblical wisdom for life and leadership.

A pioneer in the marketplace, Doc is the founder of several businesses and passionately coaches Kingdompreneurs—entrepreneurs with a Kingdom mandate—to rise as influential voices in the business world. He also leads Widman University Everywhere, a business school where aspiring entrepreneurs are trained to build impactful enterprises that advance the gospel of Jesus Christ.

Learn more at www.docmurphy.net.

Other Books and Products by Doc Murphy

The Conqueror's Mentality

S. I. Supernatural Intelligence

Accelerate

YOU Success

Dream Responsibly

Five + One

Mature

J.O.Y.

The Building Permit

The Authority of Kingdom Citizens

Personal Monetary System

Frequency

Go to Heaven

Becoming the Balanced You

Born for this

The Apostolic Church

Christian Conduct

Understanding and Discovering the Y in U

Kingdompreneur

Faith

Go Ready Set!

History Makers

Music from Mariee Murphy at www.marymurphymusic.com

Order these products @

amazon.com

APPENDIX

Paul's Thorn Continued...

For many years I have been teaching about Paul's thorn. Some receive it, and some do not. Tradition, ignorance, and man-made doctrine have kept many confused concerning this subject. As I was writing about it in this book, the Holy Spirit led me to find someone else who teaches it with more knowledge and revelation. So, I found Dr. Rick Renner (a Greek and Hebrew Scholar), and below is his superb teaching on the subject. You will enjoy this. You will be enlightened, and if you are not convinced with what I said earlier, you will be after reading Dr. Renner's teaching! – Doc Murphy

"When these two Greek words are compounded to form the word *huperairo*, it speaks of *a supremely exalted person.* This is *a person who has been magnified, increased, and lifted up to a place of great prestige and influence.* Although *huperairo* could be used to express the idea of a person who has haughtily exalted himself, this is not the idea Paul has in mind when he writes this verse. Rather, this is a person who has been greatly honored and recognized due to something he has written, done, or achieved. Notice that Paul refers to the "abundance of the revelations" that God had given to him. The word "abundance" is the Greek word *huperballo*, a compound of the word *huper*, described above, and the word *ballo*, which means *to cast* or *to throw*. But when these two words are compounded to form the word *huperballo*, it describes *something that is phenomenal, extraordinary, unparalleled, or unmatched.* It is the picture of an archer who aims for the bull's eye; but when he releases the string and shoots his arrow, he watches as his arrow flies way over the top of the target. Now Paul uses this word to explain that the revelations he had received were not only *unparalleled in quality*, but the vast number of them were *far beyond* what anyone else had ever received.

The word "revelations" is from the Greek word *apokalupsis*. It refers to *something that has been veiled or hidden for a long time and then suddenly, almost instantaneously, becomes clear and visible to the mind or eye.* It is like pulling the curtains out of the way so you can see what has always been just outside your window. The scene was always there for you to enjoy, but the curtains blocked your ability to see the real picture. But when the curtains are drawn apart, you can suddenly see what has been hidden from your view. The moment you see beyond the curtain for the first time and observe what has been there all along but not evident to you — *that* is what the Bible calls a "revelation."

From Paul's words in Second Corinthians 12:7, we know that the curtain had been pulled apart and Paul had seen into the spirit realm on many occasions.

He'd had an "abundance" of these experiences. It was this "abundance of the revelations" that Paul was preaching as he traversed the regions surrounding the Mediterranean Sea. Everywhere he went, he preached what had been divinely revealed to him. As he preached, his power, authority, and fame grew greater and greater. As his authority grew, so did his ability to impact the world with the Gospel of Jesus Christ. Due to these revelations and his boldness to preach them, Paul was unquestionably becoming one of the most influential men of his day.

Now Paul lets us know that Satan was alarmed by the great progress the apostle was making with the Gospel; therefore, the enemy launched an full-scale attack to impede that progress. Satan didn't want Paul to be recognized or magnified to a greater extent than he already was. Instead, the Devil wanted to pull down this man of God — to ruin him, to destroy him, and to discredit the message he preached. Since there was no moral flaw in Paul that Satan could use to destroy him, he inflicted Paul with a "thorn in the flesh."

The word "thorn" is the Greek word *skolops*, a word used to describe *a dangerously sharp, spiked instrument or tool.* However, this word was also used to describe *the stake on which an enemy's head was stuck after being decapitated.*

The word *skolops* gives the impression that this thorn was excruciatingly painful. Some have suggested that the words "in the flesh" refer to a physical sickness, but this is not affirmed by any scripture in the New Testament and should be taken as unsubstantiated conjecture. People have gone so far in their imaginations as to assert that Paul suffered from malaria, epilepsy, eye disease, club feet, or a hunched back. There is nothing in any New Testament scripture to back up such speculations! One thing *is* clear, however: Satan wanted Paul's head on a stake! He wanted to eliminate this man of God and put him completely out of the picture. Instead of referring to sickness, the words "in the flesh" most likely describe a type of event that was a constant source of irritation to the apostle Paul. This event caused him personal distress and kept reoccurring over and over again. For this reason, he referred to it as a "thorn in the flesh."

Some argue that God sent this thorn in the flesh to keep Paul from being prideful about his many revelations. But there is no reason to debate this issue, for Paul plainly wrote that it was a "…messenger of *Satan* to buffet me…." The word "messenger" is the Greek word *angelos*, a word that can describe *an angel; one who is sent on a special mission;* or *a messenger who is dispatched to perform a specific assignment*. This "messenger of Satan," perhaps a demonic angel, was sent directly from Satan himself to buffet Paul and to restrict the progress of his ministry.

This thorn in the flesh categorically did *not* come from God; otherwise, Paul would have called it a "messenger of God." Paul himself plainly states that this thorn in the flesh was given to him by a "messenger of Satan" — a special force that had been dispatched to keep Paul from gaining additional status and prestige and to prevent him from taking the Gospel further and higher into the world scene.

Look at the facts: Paul was preaching to kings, governors, and world leaders. He was establishing churches, writing New Testament scriptures, and pushing back the forces of hell. His personal influence was growing, and his impact was increasing day by day. The revelations that God had given him were about to change the course of human history. Fearing that Paul's influence would grow too great, Satan strategically sent forces who had been instructed to create disturbances to "buffet" the apostle.

The word "buffet" is the Greek word *kolaphidzo*, a Greek word that comes from the word *kolaphos*, a word that describes *the fist* or *knuckles*. When it becomes the word *kolaphidzo*, as Paul uses it in Second Corinthians 12:7, it refers to *beatings with the fist*. The Greek tense describes *unending, unrelenting, continuous, repetitious beatings.* This means Paul is not telling us of a single event, but of a series of many events. This word *kolaphidzo* ("buffet") gives us our greatest insight into the "thorn in the flesh" Paul is writing about in this verse.

Paul endured many afflictions during his ministry. Many of the afflictions he faced were due to the religious leaders who so fiercely opposed him. These religious leaders included Jewish leaders who hated him and his message. They also included false brethren who were constantly trying to displace his position of authority in the local churches. Paul was resisted outside the church by leaders of the Jewish faith who hated him. He was also opposed from within the church by those who wanted him out of the picture so they could take his place of prominence.

Thus, the biggest "thorn" in Paul's life was the fact that he had to deal with these different groups of people who covertly planned the problems and hassles he frequently faced in the ministry. A special messenger from Satan, perhaps even a demonic angel, had been sent to incite these people against Paul.

If you survey the types of ordeals Paul endured, you will see that many of them were orchestrated by these people who wanted to get rid of him. They were so teeming with hatred toward Paul that they wanted to see his head on a stake! These people were the primary source of Paul's problems and distractions he faced in his life and ministry.

One type of attack Paul experienced at his opponents' hands were many physical "beatings," which explains his use of the word *kolaphidzo* ("buffet") in this verse.

However, Paul was also constantly buffeted, harassed, hassled, and distracted by the negative activities of these people. As a result, he was hindered from focusing on what God had called him to do because of the great amount of time he had to spend defending his apostleship and answering the charges of those who were stirring up trouble against him. These opponents really were a thorn in the flesh for Paul. Their actions were a constant irritant that he had to deal with on an almost daily basis.

In light of these Greek words, consider this fresh interpretation of Paul's words in Second Corinthians 12:7:
"Because of the phenomenal revelations I have received and on account of the vast number of these revelations that God has entrusted to me — and to hinder the highly visible progress I am making in the Lord's cause — a special messenger has been sent from Satan to harass me with constant distractions and headaches. There's no doubt about it! Those whom Satan has stirred up against me want my head on a stake! Satan is using these people to constantly buffet and distract me in an attempt to keep me from reaching a higher level of visibility and recognition and to sidetrack me from preaching my revelations."

You see, Paul's thorn in the flesh wasn't sickness or epilepsy or any other physical malady; it was the *people* who opposed and irritated him and continually caused him problems! The Devil used these people again and again, trying to keep Paul so distracted solving "people problems" that he wouldn't be able to make any more significant personal or Gospel advancements."

- Dr. Rick Renner

Made in the USA
Coppell, TX
11 June 2025

50573903R00042